Inspirational Poetic Lyrics with Inner Meanings and Scriptures
to comfort
and encourage you
as you become...

Embraced

By

God

personalized and written by:

Sonya Nerine Hubbard

Hubbard House Publishing
Chicago, Illinois

Embraced By God

published by Hubbard House Publishing Company
Chicago, Illinois

© 2002 by Sonya Hubbard
International Standard Book Number 0-9744076-0-7

Printed in the United States of America

For information:
Hubbard House Publishing Company
Post Office Box 197
Oak Forest, Illinois 60452

Visit us on the web!
www.hubbardhousepublishing.com

This book is dedicated in the loving
memory of
Jeremy David Young,
(May 5, 2000- July 21, 2000)
Christine Harrington,
Claretha Leggett,
and
The victims of September 11, 2001.

CONTENTS

ACKNOWLEDGEMENTS

*I offer praise and recognition to my Creator.
He has cultivated words of wisdom within my soul
and has used me to spread His abundance of truth
to all mankind. His truth has touched me to share
the inner peace and joy that surrounds
and comforts me.
Thank you God for the harmony and tranquility
that you have given me through Your perfect will
and divine purpose.
To God be the glory!
I express an overflowing gratitude to my precious
grandmother, Mabel Price, for her divine grace of
encouragement. I appreciate her loyal source of
guidance and profitable judgment which stems
from her own experiences and struggles.
She endures life through her faith in God.
In the honor of my diligent and committed editor,
confidant, and life long love, my beautiful mother,
Peggy Jean Sallis-Thompson. She motivates and
inspires me with her profound wisdom
and intelligence. Her phenomenal visions
and ambitions display her honorable soul of gifted
talents that are interchangeable
through Our Father God.
I cherish my beloved son, Jamal Raheem Hubbard.
He captivates the pure essence of innocence and
integrity that embraces my soul to preserve
through challenges that allow me to achieve beyond
my limits.
He is God's special gift to me.*

The admirations of my soul, my two
beautiful sisters and best friends,
Ramona Lynn Young and Christina Rosel Sterling,
full of radiance and confidence. They stand
parallel with fortitude and vantage that impels my
essential nature to flourish.
I give thanks to my father, Wesley Thompson, Jr.,
who encourages me with his meek and keen
character. He captures an attachment of warmth
as he liberate his unconditional love to prosper
through the spirit of God.
A sincere and grateful appreciation to
Chandra Byrd-Wright and Althea Allen. You have
touched a part of my life that advocated my
expectations to excel to my greatest potential.
I would like to express a warm-hearted thank you
to Linda Carole-Pierce, Nanyamka Johnson, Angela
D. Curry-Ford, Bridget Hardy, Pollyette Love,
Lareina Davis, Brigette Maxwell, Aster Grimmage,
Dr. Leslie Best, Darryl Mitchell, Averill B. Price,
Andre D. Williams, James Hart, William Hubbard,
John Teer, and the Leggett,
Scarber, and Howard families.
I highly value and appreciate all of my relatives
and noble friends,
who contribute their constructive
criticism with faith and support.
I appreciate God's tremendous
and endless love that has drawn
a special connection with many prodigious people
who have touched my life.
Thank you, Lord. In Jesus name.
AMEN!

A Word to Embrace

A soft gentle breeze that touches
your face; it is a delicate manifestation
of God's way of communicating with you
to affirm His existence.
Before you were created you were
a spiritual conception that was
reproduced in the absence
of your existence.
You are an original and unique
pattern that God invested His creative
skills to craft a remarkable design
to fit the divine image of Him.
You are the perfect form of beauty
that features the qualities
of delight in the eyes of God.
Within the circumference
of your physical being,
lie your natural talents, gifts,
and native abilities which
are orchestrated for you to
perform and fulfill
God's ingenious and thorough plan:
His perfect will.
Reverence God for His commendable
excellence of craftsmanship;
He facilitated without
the assistance or support of others.

Chapter 1

Embraced By Grace

Blessing in Disguise

Examine deeper
than a tangible picture
of a bold, destructive, and horrific adventure.
It all started the eleventh day of September,
on this unbelievable and tragic day
that the entire nation will remember.
Full of grief and sadness,
it plays a part,
but this isn't where the story
originated
or even starts.
Lets go back
beyond the crashing of the planes,
keep in mind whose in control
the King of Heaven who reigns.
Sits on His throne
He is the King of the Earth.
Ruler of everything;
He is the creator of birth.
The Lord looks from heaven
to discriminate sin
as He watches,
He sees all
the sons of men.
From the place of His dwellings
He looks upon all the inhabitants of
the Earth.

He fashions their hearts
individually
He considers all their works.
Don't think for a second
that God doesn't know
what took place.
He governs the world
with His sovereignty grace.
Even when the enemy plots, scams, or schemes
God watches all people
regardless of the adversities or disasters.
So, don't worry about what appear
or how it may seem.
Not trying to be bold,
let the truth be told.
He's in control.
Better than gold
the power
He holds!
He knows the end before it starts.
Believe in your heart,
He's not far apart.
Your friend to the end
He lives within
lacking sin.
Dominates life!
Think again,
He'll win.
When evil occurs
as it states in the word.

*Stand with the armor
the protection of evil to seize the drama.
Are you aware
that the nation in prayer?
Something that the devil never
intended.
God turned evil inside out.
Did you comprehend it?*

God never loses. The enemy will definitely
bring on destruction to ruin God's
marvelous creation, however,
God never loses.
The enemy will persuade you to surrender
from great success to satisfy
his malicious defeats, however,
God never loses.
The enemy knows your desires.
He will attempt to prevail
against you as he causes pain or punishment
to declare the victory
in your life, however, God never loses.
God conquers, triumphs,
and gain complete power of authority.
Nothing or no one can defeat
the overpowering victory of God.
NO ONE!!!

*For whatever is born of God overcomes the world.
And this the victory that has overcomes the world,
but he who believe that Jesus is the Son of God?*

I John 5:4-5

Being Strong in the Struggle

Through my trials and obstacles,
in the midst of hardship.
To except the pain and suffering
causes a battle of conflict.
Lack of contentment without
satisfaction
no confidence or courage to gain
aspiration
induced motivation;
a created distraction.
Troubled and fulfilled
with misery and despair
"Have mercy on me"
was my only spiritual prayer.
Failure to proceed
I was ready to fall.
God was quick and noble
to reply to my call.
"Present all your worries
and problems unto me.
I am the King of Kings
the First and the Last;
cast your cares upon Me
to be set free."

Realize when you are weak
you are strong
cause the unity of Christ
in relation with God
possesses your strength to carry on.
To worry
activates positive
energy to waste.
Prayer is a seed to cultivates
that produces a birth of faith.
The name of the Lord is a strong
and mighty tower.
He is a shield of protection
He librates the power.
Refuse to worry;
focus on joy.
For the battle is not yours
It is the Lord.

**Endure means that
you must
tolerate
the conditions of life
regardless
of any situation.
Life is a
cycle of challenges.
It is up to you to
make it through
the difficult times.
Just like adversity,
prosperity is
multiple times greater
after the obstacle
course.
CHALLENGE LIFE!!!**

*Cast your burden on the Lord, and He shall sustain
you, He shall never permit the righteous to be
moved.*

Psalm 55:22

A Promissory Taken

Never failing,
it is all so real.
Not based on current circumstances
nor how you may feel.
Perfect and just in all His ways.
Vindication appears
on any God given day.
He is faithful and true,
I thought you knew.
Promise to restore justice
is never overdue.
He is faithful and just.
Seek the righteous of forgiveness
indeed
you'll be blessed.
He is faithful and fair.
Dare to stare
at the glare of God's care.
It's rare.
He'll never give you more than you can
bare.
His eye is nothing to compare
it's the symbol of tender lovin' care.

He protects from harm.
So, don't be alarmed
when the trouble comes,
just call on His only begotten Son.
Conceive to believe
that the battle of victory
is already won.
If we are faithless,
He remains faithful.
So be grateful
always thankful
of the One who causes the existence
of life and death.
Nevertheless,
God with a promise
can never deny
Himself.

> **Has someone ever made you a
> promise and this person
> could not keep it?
> Well, on the contrary, God
> promises are one hundred percent
> guaranteed. His word is a contract
> of His obligations.
> You will never have to
> worry if it is broken.
> God restores!**

*God is our refuge and strength, a very present help in
trouble. Therefore we will not fear, even though the
earth be removed, and though the mountains be
carried into the midst of the sea; through its waters
roar and be troubled, though the mountains shake
with its swelling.*

Psalm 46:1-3

Escape for Freedom

As I stand behind the gates
of my eyes and ears
with a feeling of danger
close and near.
I've decided to lock my mind
in the pillars of these towers
while I meditate on God's word
to receive strength and power.
I've been locked-up,
shackled down
for so very long.
I'm ready to break loose
absent from peace of mind,
freedom is where I belong.
I've been exempt from many desirable
conditions.
That's an error on my behalf,
I've caused that disposition
Freedom cost;
No longer fastened to the chains of fear.
Liberty!
No longer lost!
You pay the penalty to be set free.
Look at the acts
of Jesus and Ms. Tubman
with their pains and mercy.

*You have the power
to do, say, or think
as you please.
Therefore, if the Son of God
makes you free,
you shall be free indeed!*

**Freedom is having the ability to release
the fears that hinders your faith.
Shielding your fear
can cause perplexities in your life
that could limit your ability to strive
for perfection.
To become set free means to exercise
your common rights
and your God-given privileges
to submit to the restrictions
that keep you confined
from moving ahead.
Conquer fear and apply your faith.**
Let Go and Let God!

*For when you were slaves of sin, you were free in regard to
righteousness. What fruit did you have then in the things
of which you are now ashamed? For the end of those things is
death. But now having been set free from sin, and having
become slaves of God, you have your fruit to holiness, and the end,
everlasting life. For wages of sin is death, but the gift of
God is eternal life in Christ Jesus our Lord.*

Romans 6:20-22

Victory is Granted in the Praise

It's a shame
what the devil attempts to use in vain.
Never withstand the chance
of the tricks from the enemies' plan.
A conceived thought of deception
is what the enemy attempts to choose.
To deviate from the plan
for God's child to be used.
Just like Job
when times got rough
a plead for contentment.
God's reply...
"enough is enough."
On a daily and consistent circumstance,
on bended knees with closed hands,
praise and thank the Lord
using all you can.
He lives in you.
He is alive!
Cherish and appreciate
all the wonderful things
He offers and provides.
He is full of wisdom and knowledge
with dominion and grace.

He loves you unconditionally,
as you stand on faith.
Be weary for nothing
believe in His word.
Be thankful for everything,
even when trouble proceeds to occur.
Never underestimate
the power of God's grace,
it is given for you
to embrace.
Haste is waste
when you wander in space.
So, don't create a disgrace
as you plead for God to take His place.
So enter into His presence
with thanksgiving and praise.
Reverence Him in worship
to please His Holy and Righteous name.

The favor of God, plus the love of God,
equals the grace from God.
God's grace is an unconditional gift
given to all men,women, and children.
This elegant form of beauty with divine
excellence is what blesses us
from day to day.
It showers our lives to express the power
of God's tender mercy and kindness.
When you pray it becomes
a special connection with God.
It unifies a system of communication
that allows God to receive your gift.
Reverence and honor Him.
Reap your gift of grace, from God,
as you sow God's gift through prayer.

*Oh, give thanks to the Lord, for He is good! For His mercy
endures forever. Who can utter the mighty acts of the Lord?
Who can declare all His praise? Blessed are those who keep
justice, And he who does righteousness at all times!*
Psalms 106:1-3

Anchor Your Soul

Think for a moment,
as I relate to the everlasting story
given by Moses
from Almighty God.
Alliance to the affirmed commandments
of laws
to His loyal people
that were separated from fraud.
When you abide, tolerate, and remain in
His truth,
a covenant of submission
with yielding
reveals God's identity of proof.
In other words,
when you believe and obey
His word of the law.
Faith will show up,
perfect
like Jesus
awesome
without a flaw.
Obedience determines your blessings acquired.
Which do you prefer
favor or curses?
Depends on what your heart desires.
Comply to act in the accordance
of God's voice.

Conceive to the fact
that the Lord's blessings
are the only obtainable source.
The love for God
is more than just a conscious feeling;
In the act of obedience,
which do you select to be more appealing?
The Lord God will make you the head
and not the tail.
If you obey faithfully
using His Word,
achieve the purpose of victory to prevail.
You shall be above only
and not become beneath,
because the supreme spirit of evil
knows that his full power of control
lies beneath your feet.
Turn to Jesus and repent all your sins.
Ask the Lord to come into your heart
to be your Almighty Friend.
With God in your life
you'll be set free
to pure justification.
So don't deviate to the plan of the enemy
for an inadequate soul gratification.
Ask God to renew and change
your heart.

*This is where salvation
and deliverance usually starts.
Allow and permit
the Lord to come in
as you read and believe
in His Word.
This is were it usually begins.
Don't conform your mind to this
unrighteous universe.
God's a living Spirit,
on the contrary
He's not diverse.
So use your bodies to serve
and obey God.
Remind your soul
that it's the master
of your physical control.
Plant and establish
yourself in God sovereignty.
He's The Omniscient;
there's nothing greater than He!*

Your soul is a shadow that exists
in your physical structure.
It is an essential ingredient composed
of thoughts, feelings, and actions
that are considered to be
the spiritual portion
of the human body.
It survives death
that would proceed
to contentment or poverty
in the following life.
Our soul is a fundamental tool
that is devoted and connected
to God's entity.
Allow God to chauffeur your soul
as you take your journey through life.
As you travel,
He will be your Provider,
your Leader, and Friend.
A compass is not required.

someone turns him back, let him know that he who turn a
sinner from the error of his way will save a soul from
death and cover a multitude of sins.

James 5:19-20

*What a perfect form of
beauty, elegance, and a pleasing
charm that God bestows upon us;
His Grace.*

*He gives us mercy and favor to
allow His perfect will to shine
through mankind. We are
mirrors that reflect His perfect
image that glows brilliantly to
please His domains;*
The Kingdom of Heaven.

Chapter 2

Embraced By Faith

She Touched "Hem"

In the world she trusted
when she searched for a cure.
By whose stripes you were healed
stated plain and pure.
Times were rough
yet with the familiar surface.
Unyielding and aimed
for a firm of purpose.
She crawled among the crowd
in an agitated town.
Searched with loyalty
without a sound
only one thought in mind;
dependence for a touch
of the Holy Gown!
Having belief without
an attainable proof.
One goal intended,
encouraged to stand aloof.
Don't allow the flesh to suppress
the power of God.
Determined,
eagerly
with a purpose
she plod.

Sadness and depression
was held captive
to be cast down.
No time to search the past
to bring abound.
One change she was willing to make
every step closer
inspired to break
the tedious ache.
On a path
she was ruthless and doubtless
to take.
A chance for healing
a sacrifice of sake.
Approaching slowly
with all hope in her hand.
At last!
She touch the man
who heals the land.
In a moment,
that very instant,
she was set free.
Rose with abundance of faith
from her bended knees.
Transferred power released,
favor availed.
"Be in good cheer,
your faith has made you well.
Go in peace," as she refused for faith to fail.

Are you confident, but yet afraid?
Do you have feelings of self-assuredness,
but apprehensive? Sure opposites may
attract in some cases, however, faith
and fear can not reside in the same space.
They can not unite to accomodate our
deepest desires. Faith stands isolated
without the acknowledgement of fear.
When you step out on faith you are walking
on dependence, trust, confidence, security,
and reliance for God to accomplish
your delightful vision.

"Because of your unbelief; for assuredly, I say to you, if you
have faith as a mustard seed, you will say to this mountain,
'Move from here to there' and it will move;
and nothing will be impossible for you.
However, this kind does not go out except
by prayer and fasting."
                                        Matthew 17:20-21

In the Fiery Furnace

Are you focusing your mind
on problems instead of power?
Don't worship the rulers
of the darkness
and allow the true word to go sour.
Is your troubled mind based
on fear instead of faith?
Don't allow the devil
to creep in
and allow your true destiny to go to waste.
Would you rather concentrate
on sin instead of our Saviour?
The power,
it's a given
take heed, conceive, and give labor.
Are you worried and annoyed
by troubles instead of triumphs?
Don't give up
give in,
fall victim to sin
then eventually deny Him!
Sometimes we are placed
in situations that are not meant to be.
During a moment of weakness
ask, seek, knock;
Jesus holds the key.

From the works
of Shadrach, Meshach, and Abedego,
they didn't only have faith,
they waited for the Redeemer to show!
So regardless of what the situation
may display.
Be obedient and follow
the instructions of the Lord.
That's the only way!

**Feelings are based on
a sense of tangible experiences.
Faith is not the foundation
of your feelings.
However it is a seed of expectancy
for authentic loyalty that is
planted in a spiritual substance.**

*Verily I say unto you, If ye have faith, and doubt not, ye shall
not only done this which is done to the fig tree, but also if ye
shall say unto this mountain, Be thou removed, and be thou
cast into the sea; it shall be done. And all things, whatsoever
ye shall ask in prayer, believing, ye shall receive.*

Matthew 21:21-22

Skin: The Baggage You Live In

It's over now.
Do you still feel the pain?
You've been through
hail, snow, and even rain.
What about the feelings
that come from above?
They are created and made
from God
with love.
People think hurt
is emotion from sin.
Remember, God is the Creator,
so think again and again.
The pain that you feel inside
derives
from hurt,
deal with it,
don't run and hide.
Pain is made of thoughts and memories
in you mind.
Just understand
to get over it,
is a matter of time.
It's similar to having the flu
to get through the pain
take some medicine
and take care of "you".

Don't allow the pain
to take over your life,
this advocates the devil
with his weapon of strife.
Heal yourself
as you stand on His word.
Consistent prayer causes deliverance,
prevail to emerge.
Always remember
the life you have
is yours to keep.
Until God says its over
and pronounces...
eternally sleep.
But in the meantime,
while it's in your possession,
dominate your life
even through
your transgressions!
God will never give up on you.
Communion with the Father
it's the most revolutionary thing to do!

Pain from affliction is an effective
weapon from the enemies objective.
Whether the pain is emotional or
physical this can cause a delay of
procession in your life.
Don't allow pain to
be the obstruction
that deters your
goals and ambitions.
Don't throw in the towel
and surrender without a fair fight.
Pain is the major process
in achieving the greatest reward.
A newborn baby is the
reward to a mother
that suffered childbirth.
Salvation is the reward
from the suffering of
Jesus' crucifixion.
So, whatever your reward is
remember pain will be one
of the instruments that
help facilitate your
greatest performance.
ENDURE THOUGH THE PAIN!

*And we know that all things work together for
good to them that love God, to them who are the called
according to his purpose.*

Romans 8:28

Disguised in the Presence of God

Pure observation is what he used.
Once upon a time
stationed in heaven.
Consume to amuse
by using musical tools.
Full of hate, envy, wrath,
and strife
cast down
far beneath the ground
for an extremely
unpleasant eternal life.
With thoughts of a rebellious
and a defiant heart
reflecting feelings of violence
from being expelled,
separated,
and apart.
Determined to defeat and conquer the Earth
using negative skills
to gain power
over the entire universe;
this useless power attempts
to operate in every physical form.
Declares to be the ruler
of the Earth.

Hated you
the moment you were born.
Strong desires to punish
every series of events
that takes place or transpires.
Knows your heart;
beware of the ruthless secret admirer.
Restricts you from obtaining
the powerful word
from the Book of knowledge.
He wants you lost, ruined,
and eventually abolished.
Strives to confuse
your main business,
occupation, or hobby.
Using a dishonest attempt
to make the imitation
the genuine or original copy.
Get on guard,
as a sign of warning and danger,
because the "father of lies"
is not a visitor or guest.
He is worse than a stranger.
He's not concealed in a mask
to protect and cover
his unrighteous character.
He comes to capture your soul
as a wicked sorcerer player.

Satan, the king of evil,
transforms your faith to false.
Maintain the Word knowledge
consistently.
Don't go astray,
wonder off, and get lost.
As you pray and read
the power of God's word,
His presence will show.
Listen, perceive, and take heed
to what you heard.
So be strong in the Lord
and the power of His might.
Eliminate the devil
and his evil line of attacks
out of your life.

Satan, the adversary of God,
has no power at all.
His counterfeit powers are only powerful
when you choose to give them to him.
The devil tries to interfere
with your divine purpose for the will of God.
If you allow Satan to intervene in your life,
this permits his powers to prevail.
Corresponding with God on a consistent
and daily basis allows
the enemies' cruel plots to become limited.
Achieve victory over the enemy
by acknowledging God through prayer
with supplication and eliminate
the acknowledgements of the enemies
weapons of dishonesty, trickery, and deceit.
Understand, Satan can not exist
without your permission.

If God is for us, who can be against us?

Romans 8:31

In the Sanctuary

As I sit in this holy temple
of guided pasturing.
Listening to God's word,
preaching...
and some good choir singing.
I look around in this grand worship service,
my heart ponders
at the amount of people
who may be unsaved...
then immediately I get nervous.
Can I maintain focus
and discern God's calling?
Or ignore God
and allow the demonic angels
to start falling?
As a child of God,
it is my duty to obey and serve God;
the Ruler.
According to Acts 1:8
we are His people
who received power
and lead to witness.
Don't get scared.
It's time to build up your spiritual walk
and get down to God's business.
We must go forth
to defeat the unbeatable odds.

*It's His kingdom
that He's concerned about.
Come with the victory
and glorify God.
Pray unto the Lord
using knowledge and wisdom
sacrifice sin.
Exalt His awesome and precious kingdom.*

> **God's spiritual composition is love, joy, peace, longsuffering, kindness, goodness, faithlessness, gentleness and self-control. All of these attributes are a combination of one characteristic given freely. Worship God with enthusiasm through song and dance to show appreciation of God's worth.**

*Do you know that our body is the
temple of the Holy Spirit who is in you, whom you have from
God and you are not your own? For you were brought at a
price, therefore glorify God in your body and in your spirit
which are God's.*

I Corinthians 6:19-21

Surrounded By "Aints" Who Act Like Saints

Who do they think they are?
Saved and sanctified
HUMMM???
Not by far.
It kills me
how you praise and worship.
As I say to myself
"man 'ain't' they a trip."
Trying so hard
to be somebody you're not.
Ask,
Holy Spirit,
is that something I got?
Jumping around giving
God phony shouts.
The devil is present.
Did you know
without a doubt?
Sit and listen to pastor preach
as he teach
for three consecutive sermons on his feet.
Well, I guess His word
doesn't serve a purpose
'cause there are saints
in the process of showing a disservice.

Walking around with a bible in hand,
trying hard to convince...
'God is the man with the master plan'
and you're accountable
as you explain,
The Bible says you must not worship
His name in vain.
As you proclaim
that your Father above
is your number one choice.
Is this deception,
or did you really discern His voice?
Impressive
with your artificial word knowledge.
Majored in theology
when you went to college?
The word you seem to know so well.
So does the "father of sin"
who resides in hell.
Perhaps he may know it better than you.
It's hard to tell
the way you scheme
and tell lies, too.
A spiritual lifestyle is what you portray.
As I can see,
you rather do it your way.
Did you know that we are not our own?
We are brought with a price
so leave me alone!

The church is a place where Christians
fellowship to worship God.
The human body is the domain in which
Christ resides.
In conjunction, each structure forms a
sacrificial purpose to create a spiritual
bondage to God.
Failure to operate in the life
that was not intended from God is
immoral. The duty of a believer is to act in
a Godly manner during church service and
abroad. God's presence not only resides
in the church, a holy temple,
but in your body, a physical temple.
So do not underestimate the two,
for they are both considered
the House of God's Temple.

Do not be unequally yoked together with unbelievers.
For what fellowship has righteousness with lawless-
ness? And what communion has light with dark-
ness?...For you are the temple of the living God. As
God has said: "I will dwell in them and walk among
them. I will be their God. And they shall be
My people."

II Corinthians 6:14,16

God's definite promises are never
failing. All of the set principles and
beliefs that He promised are evidence
of faith. His loyal obligations of
truth are consistent and reliable.
God will do exactly what He says.
You must stand steadfast
in attachment with His Word.
Do not allow logical facts and
material experiences to become
the affirmation of your faith.
Faith is the substance of things hoped
for, the evidence of things not seen.
Allow patience to comfort
you as you stand in faith.

Chapter 3

Embraced By Courage

The Backslider

I've fallen back in sin.
Lost hope and faith.
Can I get back up again?
My strong desires
allowed me to creep into the unrighteous,
but with repentance and prayer
God might just...
Oh no!
I did it again!
Feel so convicted
I want this sin to end.
What should I do?
Drop it like a bad habit and...
"I'm running back to you"
I've been dishonest and a liar.
If I remain on this path
eventually I'll be cast
into the lake of fire.
Sin,
that's not part of God spiritual structure.
He's all about
obedience and truth,
that's His culture.
I can't continue and subject my life
to doing wrong.
Must convert,
praise God,

and sing the...
"hallelujah songs".
In my heart
this is something that I don't want to do,
but in my mind,
this battle is so hard
to break through.
Hold up,
oh no!
There I go again!
I'm slippin',
trippin',
my soul is rippin' in two.
I know God don't like ugly
now what am I suppose to do?
In a moment
of spiritual unconsciousness.
I'm possessed
in the pleasure of this foolishness.
The fear of God's power
is slowly trickling in.
Maybe I'll fall back
where I use to stand
and that's seeking God's face
and not His hand.
Cause you see,
He never left
always willing to converge.

I turned my back
with a detachable urge.
This vigorous stronghold
I was willing to end,
'Cause there's hell to pay.
The consequence of sin.

Regardless of any situation,
God loves you!
Count on Him when
you fall victim to the enemy's trap.
Do not focus or invest
your thoughts to manifest a sense
of conviction. God holds
no halo of condemnation
over your crown.

If we say that we have no sin, we deceive ourselves, and
the truth is not in us. If we confess our sins He is
faithful and just to forgive us our sins and to cleanse us
from all unrighteousness.

I John 1:8-9

*I*nnocent Eyes

*The words that would fall
from his lips!
Receptive to my ears
and inner place.
Impressive,
that's where he sits.
Opened world!
I've decided to give so freely.
Couldn't acknowledge
that it all belongs to me.
Moving fast
without
withdrawals or regrets.
At times,
indecisive about commitment
due to petty mess.
Overlooked the pain
by the immeasurable amount
of physical and gentle pleasures.
Touch my soul with a delicate,
but intense and unbelievable measure.
Thoughts of you
reside in my heart.
Longed for your physical-
yeah,
your distinctive mark.*

Another level
you were willing to go-
Hesitation!
My mouth says yes,
but my heart
says **no**.
Something didn't feel so right,
the fear of darkness
no sight of light.
Wrapped in sin,
can't let it end.
Let's start again
at the point of being friends.
Exclude the function
of reproduction.
Interact with Spirit
through our repercussion.
Repent, seek, and pray for forgiveness.
Obey the Lord
for an eternal position.
Refusion on your behalf,
want to continue
on this unrighteous path?
I can't believe that you won't let it go.
Do you believe
that you reap what you sow?
I must proceed to receive a blessing.
To follow on your path
will be a horrible lesson.

No matter how bad
I may feel.
I must continue
with my desirable zeal.
God's way of life is what I choose.
I must obey God
and follow His rules.
You've deceived,
mislead and taken from me.
I made a spiritual choice
to set you free.

Beware of how you may allow
others to take authority of your life.
You must cover every area
of your existence by using
prayer and discernment as a tool
of protection against
the perils of betrayal or deceit.
Establishing a one on one relationship
with God advocates self-awareness
and this allows you to have a better
grip on your life
to eliminate vulnerable influences.

Do not be deceived, my beloved brethren.
Every good gift and every perfect gift is from
above,

                        James 1:16-17

Trust

It's hard to believe
in someone who
has done you wrong.
A special place
in my heart
all of a sudden
you don't belong.
Walked in my life
touched it
with love and belief.
Now a rejected heart
from betrayal and deceit.
Want so badly to make it right
everything said and done
I don't take so light.
So clever in ways
that I never thought existed-
unfair influences;
captivator,
you couldn't resist it.
Do you take me
for some type of game?

Heart breaker,
manipulator,
ought to change your name.
Mr. Lame?
Need to be taught and tamed.
That's a shame
you don't consider
yourself the blame!
Broke my peace
and comfort position.
You're so wrong,
no remorse
you were on a mission.
Now reluctant to depend
and rely on you.
I thought that you'd be a part
of my dream come true.
No commitment
lack of confidence
I had no expectation of another.
I wouldn't doubt it
if you deceived your own mother.
What is a person
that can't hold the truth?
Be sincere
to self first,
you don't care
so what's the use?

The foundation for any successful relationship is trust. The confidence that we deposit in someone or that we seek from others is relinquished through God. So before you begin to surrender your trust, first, receive permission from God to recognize the trust in others.

Trust in the Lord with all thine-heart; and lean not unto thine own understanding. In all thy ways acknowledge him, and he shall direct thy paths.
Proverbs 3:5-6

Satan Becomes Saviour

Fear, hatred, pain, deceit,
misery, lies, anger, lack of peace.
Is it part of your soul?
Is it mine or is it yours?
What do you do when these
emotions creep up on you?
Should you worship
these "little children"
birthed from the
"father of sin",
or frisk it at the door
and don't let it in?
How do you react
to Satan's chit-chatter?
Do you reply with anger
and accept the pain,
or does it really matter?
Pray to God for recovery,
as you stand, believe, and trust.
Have faith in God
for wholeness
that's a MUST!
With God in your life
He'll defeat
the biggest battle
or leave it up to Satan or
does it really matter?

Did you know that
satan hates you?
Oh yeah,
he hates your guts!
Put on God's word
and kick him in the butt!
Put on the whole armor
and mess him up!
Don't dare turn
from sane to sin.
Ignore the devil,
allow his power to end.
You have more power than he.
Open God's book,
read,
acknowledge
you'll see.
The "father of sin"
is a defeated foe.
You've got the power!
Did you know,
did you know?
He tries so hard
to prove his powerless ways.
As we fall victim
to his earthy and evil days.
Don't fall in his trap of "tricknowledgy".
Keep in mind
that there is something greater than he.

Except the fact and don't deny
repeat this
its me,
I'm greater than he!
Be diligent
and know that
you can't serve
something that is less than you.
Give up the horoscopes and psychics, too.
Never 'laxed,
laid back,
always on duty.
His job is to kill, steal, and destroy;
he's defiled and rudely.
Before you know it
you're laid up in sin
praising your father...
NO!
Now your best friend.
He'll convert you from God
discerns you deep into sin.
He wants you dead
and hating God.
Not born again!
In one breath
and my own opinion,
the devil is defeated,
he has no dominion!

Satan does not wear a physical disguise,
he exists in all types of personalities.
He carries emotional
and social characteristics of an
individual that conforms to ones
practical preference. Get on guard
against the deception and clever
acts designed to amuse you for a
horrible set-up of destruction
in your life. Having God
as your confidant weeds
out all possibilities
of the satanic forces that
camouflages your
practical ideas, views, and vision.

Be strong in the Lord and the power of his might.
Put on the whole armour of God, that ye may be
able to stand against the wiles of the devil.
For we wrestle not against flesh and blood,
but against principalities, against powers,
against spiritual wickedness in high places.
Wherefore take unto you the whole arnour of God,
that ye maybe able to withstand the evil day,
and having done all,
to stand.

Ephesians 6:10 -12

Hold Please!!!

Wait!
Dare not to participate.
Your rebound
could result
in a moment of hate.
When your desire
comes before the improper time.
When you give up to quickly,
the aggression
causes a crime
in your mind.
Think with less obscurity
a rebellious decision
opens the door
to the identity of hypocrisy.
Be still and stand.
Watch the power of God;
the perfection of beauty
is in His hands.
God is the only
spiritual option.
The enemy comes in
for a demonic adoption.
Timing and patience
is an extremely important part
of organization.

Wait!
Transmitting is in the process
to receive
a complete authorization.
If you move to fast
and choose not to wait,
you'll end up with counterfeit
and cause your true blessings
to be late.
Those who wait on the Lord
shall renew their strength.
The Lord gives power
to those who have faith
and trust in Him.
At times it seems
the wicked receives
a great amount of prosperity.
As God reminds us
that they will be cut off
with a little less integrity.
The meek shall
inherit the earth.
A given succession
before any physical birth.

God's creation
has been established and assigned.
He will manifest glory
in His own due time.
God is going to release
whatever He wants you to receive.
God shall supply all your needs
as you stand with patience
and have faith
as you believe.

Waiting can make you feel hasten
to react to things that are not feasible
to your situation. Having the ability to cope
with time is having the ability to tolerate
the circumstances that are being
challenged or endured in a defined
period of time. Patience is conducive to
success and success is conducive
to attaining the wealth, high reward,
and exceptional achievement
by using great effort and courage
in spite of obstacles and disadvantages.

Wait on the Lord; Be of good courage, and He shall
strengthen your heart: Wait, I say, on the Lord!
Psalm 27:14

What gives us courage?
Fear.
That's right, without fear
you would not be able to
gain the ability to attain courage.
Courage enables us to face
difficulty, danger, and pain.
Without fear
courage can not be permitted,
however, God ascribes
courage within us.
Prayer dominates
the abilities to conquer fear
and develop the power
to produce courage.

Chapter 4

Embraced By Peace

Stuck in the "Whale"

I'm alone
and feel the need
to be needed.
The feeling of emptiness
something succeeded.
Did I make this particular choice?
Stuck in wildness
says, God's voice.
Must realize
the Spirit brought me here.
Knowing God
will never leave, nor forsake,
no doubt, no fear.
So you must stand
in the middle of wilderness,
because it builds character
and lower humbleness.
Wilderness
is a test of trail.
To build your strength
you must endure
regardless of the measurements
and lengths.
Jonah sat in the wilderness
with the presence of God.

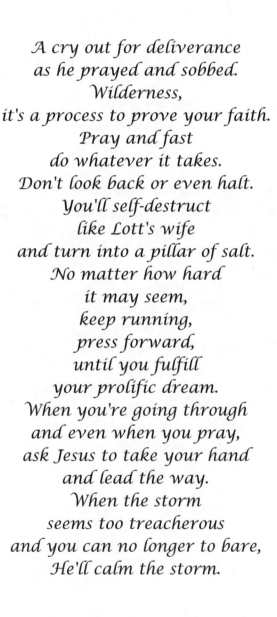

A cry out for deliverance
as he prayed and sobbed.
Wilderness,
it's a process to prove your faith.
Pray and fast
do whatever it takes.
Don't look back or even halt.
You'll self-destruct
like Lott's wife
and turn into a pillar of salt.
No matter how hard
it may seem,
keep running,
press forward,
until you fulfill
your prolific dream.
When you're going through
and even when you pray,
ask Jesus to take your hand
and lead the way.
When the storm
seems too treacherous
and you can no longer to bare,
He'll calm the storm.

Trust Him,
He'll be there.
God will see you through
as you end with a splendid
testimony
and an awesome
break-through!

So, you have been sentenced to solitude. Exclusively without the presence of humanity. In this place of concealment is a place where character, low self-esteem, and self-complacency can be harvested. Lacking the company of others is perpetual travel to get more acquainted with your essential nature that will establish your self-identity. This process may cause you to detach yourself from others in order to connect with yourself and God.

But seek ye first the kingdom of God,
and his righteousness; and all these
things shall be added to you.
Matthew 6:33

There's Life in the Blood

The choice was made
thirty-three years later
He rose from the grave.
Created from the Father
sinless and meek
healing take place
the moment He speaks.
On a mission
to save us from immortal sin
delegated to win
using the power within:
His skin.
Shed the blood
to disperse The Power.
No longer will the devil
have control to consume or devour
from his obnoxious, crude,
and mystical power.
Salvation was birthed
and you're born again,
you are now safe, secured,
and delivered from sin.
The right hand of God
reverted to the throne.

*No struggles or danger
and you're no longer alone.
As the Comforter
which resides within,
He will continue to guide you
and you must remember
He is your Lord, Saviour, and Friend.*

The cross: a wooden instrument
for torment. Due to Jesus' crucifixion
and the sacrificing of His blood
He has given us an opportunity
to communicate closer to God in the
most intimate and exalting way.
Salvation is God's way of allowing
all of humanity to benefit from
the source of Jesus resurrection.
The soul has an everlasting existence.
There is an eternal destiny beyond life
and it is proven precisely from
Jesus' resurrection. Symbolically and
surrealistically speaking, the cross
represents the commitment to do
the will of God. Therefore, take up
your cross daily to resemble Jesus'
willingness to do God's will.

*The Lord is my light and my salvation; Whom shall I fear?
The Lord is the strength of my life; Of whom shall I be
afraid?*

Psalm 27:1

Console My Physical

Ease the grief
or sorrow
of my discomfort.
My desires of joy and peace
are swallowed within myself.
I yearn for another type of pleasure
that makes my heart pump faster.
Increases the sound
of my drive and laughter.
I'm in the mood for smiling,
profiling
as my body switches
to a more comfortable position.
Once on my back,
now on my side,
as I see the perfect view before me.
I'm anxious to know the very next move.
I'm so excited
that it keeps falling out my hand!
Don't want to lose it;
forget this position
I'm ready to stand.
My ears are receptive to the sounds
of the rhetoric.
I can't believe how this is making me feel.

As my body consumes
to the pleasure-
Oh fantastic!
I began to jump around,
moan and groan.
As the happiness
enters my soul.
Suddenly the spirit takes over
and my physical is out of control.
This feeling of satisfaction
seems to have
full power of authority.
As I climax
and brought back
to my first priority.
Receiving God's word
as I stay home.
Being ministered from the T.V.
and realizing---
I'm not alone.

God's compassion for us is so
stimulating that it inspires your soul
to elevate to a level of ecstacy.
A whisper to God in prayer, activates
the love that He has for us that
presents itself in many ways.
Delight yourself in pleasing God
though the prayer of
praise and worship.

For those who live according to the flesh
set their minds on the things of the flesh,
but those who live according to the Spirit,
the things of the Spirit. For to be carnally
minded is death, but to be
spiritually minded is life and peace.
Romans 8:5-6

Serenity Principle

What a relief
I've finally found peace
drifting in space
awaiting for me
to capture, hold, caress,
and embrace
in this matchless place.
An infinite pleasure
to grasp for eternity
forget about loneliness
it just you and me:
peace.
Standing free
on the edge of the universe
holding hands
permitting good to convert
from worse
losing myself
in this deep hollow form
no time for fear
its prayer that keeps me
snuggly warm.

Obscurity of love,
and the rage of joy
has opened up
to reveal it true identity
into a sweet supernatural form
of reality.
No longer living a dream
of an illusion
that seems so real.
Walking in peace
as confusion stands still.

One may have the tendency to think that peace is discovered initially from the perimeter of your inner being. On the contrary, it lies in the nucleus of your soul. It is shared with the perfect unity of harmony, comfort, and love. It is the recognition of true happiness and intangible prosperity. It is the healing and forgiveness of past pains. It is the true awareness of God's presence.

And the peace of God, which surpasses all understanding, will guard our hearts and minds through Christ Jesus.
Philippians 4:7

Be Real

I wish
that I could end
this horrible pain
'cause I already know
we don't have anything to gain.
I allow you to be a part of my life.
I even consider
for you to take my hand
to be your wife.
You deceived me
and betrayed me with sin.
I can't even trust you
to be a close friend.
You took me through hell
with your own foolish mess.
Hate I ever met you,
but eventually I'll be blessed.
So please stay out of my life
and leave me alone.
'Cause you're nothing but trouble.
I should have **been** gone.
Continue to give you
the benefit of the doubt,
tried to work it out,
especially at night.
Got caught up in sin
with your wicked lust.

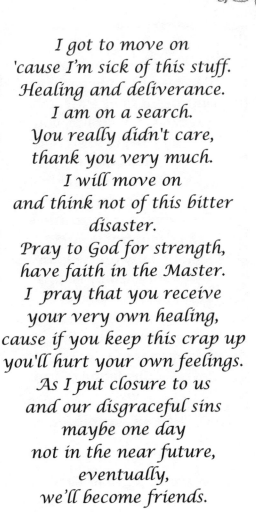

I got to move on
'cause I'm sick of this stuff.
Healing and deliverance.
I am on a search.
You really didn't care,
thank you very much.
I will move on
and think not of this bitter
disaster.
Pray to God for strength,
have faith in the Master.
I pray that you receive
your very own healing,
cause if you keep this crap up
you'll hurt your own feelings.
As I put closure to us
and our disgraceful sins
maybe one day
not in the near future,
eventually,
we'll become friends.

After being hurt or deceived by someone you considered to be extremely precious in your life, you may begin to set expectations that would secure your vulnerable environment. Protecting our insecurities to refrain from getting emotionally bruised can be established by setting boundaries. God is a perfect asset in assisting and assembling the boundaries of your life to navigate the nature of true love.

You shall set bounds for the people all around...

Exodus 19:12

The Domains of Darkness-Depleted

Four equal angles
that deciphers a room.
I'm pushed and force
in a corner
like a student in time out
that has been ill-mannered,
rude,
or impolite
I assume.
Surrounded with no window
enclosed in the dark.
Afraid of the faith
as my life falls apart.
Where is the door that leads to escape?
I keep forgetting
it's my mind that's in bondage
as I fail to relate.
Peace be still!
Repeal and heal
what I feel
as I reveal
my skills
to live
for the sake of God's will.

Joy is rendered
as I choose to surrender
from the devil's hidden agenda
that hinders
my inner
thoughts
that subjects a sinner
to fall victim
to his imperfect faults.
I won't depend
on life to bring me joy;
with the presence of God,
I will employ the joy
to bring me life
and give me life
forever more.

Regardless of the external surfaces, for you to
reach the utmost limits of joy and peace depend
on you. How determined are you to seek beyond
the inner softness of peace that lies beneath your
agitated afflictions? The enemy attempts to
cultivate disturbances so that your crop of
freedom from strife, of any kind, is rejected.
You will find serenity at the base of confusion.
Dig it up! Pray.

No weapon that is formed against thee shall prosper;
and every tongue that rises against thee
in judgment thou shalt condemn.
Isaiah 54:1

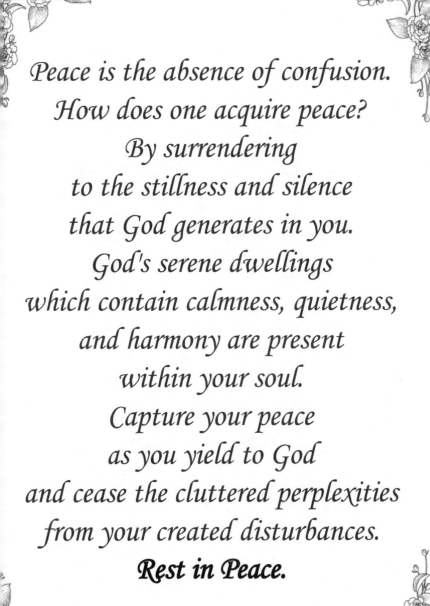

Peace is the absence of confusion.
How does one acquire peace?
By surrendering
to the stillness and silence
that God generates in you.
God's serene dwellings
which contain calmness, quietness,
and harmony are present
within your soul.
Capture your peace
as you yield to God
and cease the cluttered perplexities
from your created disturbances.

Rest in Peace.

Chapter 5

Embraced By a Gentle Touch

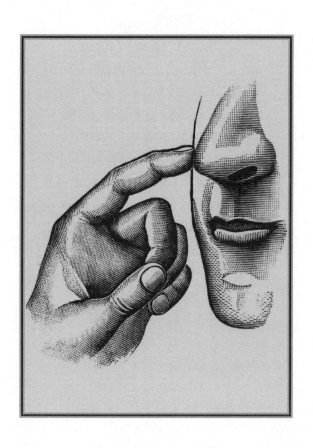

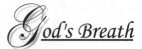od's Breath

I remember when it touched me.
In an instant I was set free.
Being on my knees,
praying for wisdom
and knowledge to see.
Everything began
to work in my favor.
It amazed me
when I accepted Jesus
as my Lord and Saviour.
All of a sudden
I felt dead wrong,
'cause the favor I had
was consumed and gone.
Thinking in my mind,
how did I lose God?
A puzzled feeling
felt kind of odd.
Pray harder.
Plead to my Father,
to come back.
to be a part of my life.
Don't lack.
I'll try to be right.

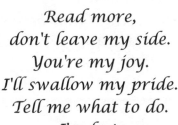

Read more,
don't leave my side.
You're my joy.
I'll swallow my pride.
Tell me what to do.
I'm lost.
I need a word from you.
Turned and tossed;
the cost.
I will sacrifice to pay,
any day
for You to come my way.
Steadfast; count not my past.
Hold on.
I'll be strong.
In the midst of my winter
the wind blows,
but I never get cold.
Obey.
Did I hear Him say?
"I never left"
The touch of God's breath.
He granted me grace.
Tears vanished from my face.
In whom I will trust
He's faithful and just.

From this day on
renew born.
Understand and believe
that the Almighty God
will never leave.

The breath of God is a symbol of His
royal power and bountiful presence.
The touch of God's gentle love reigns
upon all of His creation. Rest assure
that the presence of God is so
comforting that it grasps our soul
and strengthens our weakness.
God is the source of
fulfillment, hope, courage,
prosperity and ultimately as well as
importantly, love.

I will hear what God the Lord will speak,
for He will speak peace to His
people and to His saints;

                    Psalm 85:8

Surrender

You may be traveling down
a difficult road.
This walk may seem long,
lonely, bitter, and cold.
Never give up
and you must not quit,
'cause I'm sure this walk
with God
is nothing
more than for your benefit.
God's road never comes to an end.
He will direct your life,
because He choose
to be your Almighty Friend.
Suddenly another stumbling block
hinders your way.
It's God in the midst
who has the final say.
He supplies all your needs
He replies to your prayers.
Trust in the Lord,
because He will never give you
more than your soul can bare.
During the moment of weakness,
which is only for a season.

God is on your side regardless
of the circumstances,
situations, or reasons.
So after you have done
all that you can.
Take His hand
to end the pain.
Continue to pray
as you call on His name
you will become delivered,
but you must stay strong
and maintain as you stand.
He will lead you
just where He wants you to be.
He is the answer
and
His love is free!

When we surrender
we give admission to
submission. Giving up or
letting go is not a sign of
weakness, it is having the
ability to rely on God to
direct us on the right path.
When we are weary, He
provides the means of
strength. When we are
frightened, He finds a way
through with encourage-
ment. When we are lost, He
gently leads with clarity.
Release your ticket to God
for the removal of obstacles.

Therefore submit to God. Resist the
devil and he will flee from you.
Draw near to God and He will draw
near to you. Cleanse your hands, you
sinners; and purify your
hearts...Humble yourselves in the
sight of the Lord, and He will lift
you up.
                    James 4: 7-10

If I Only Have God-That's Enough

I don't want to look at me
to discover in the mirror
what I see.
Bringing in remembrance
the day of death.
A tear drop falls
as I take a deep breath.
To understand
the full potential
inside
love, joy, peace,
I must conquer to rise.
God loves me,
this is so.
A touch from heaven
as He looks below.
I will move on
and keep the faith.
Hang on to God
as He does with His grace.
I will press through
and be a success,
God's presence appears
as I progress.

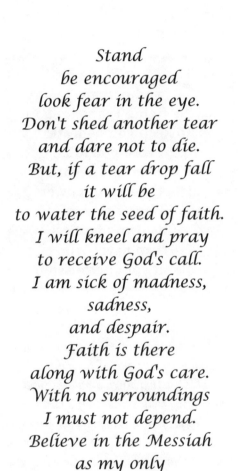

Stand
be encouraged
look fear in the eye.
Don't shed another tear
and dare not to die.
But, if a tear drop fall
it will be
to water the seed of faith.
I will kneel and pray
to receive God's call.
I am sick of madness,
sadness,
and despair.
Faith is there
along with God's care.
With no surroundings
I must not depend.
Believe in the Messiah
as my only
true friend.

Look fear in the face
and prepare
for the fight! Fear tries hard
to keep you beneath
your greatest potential, but
remember this negative
disbelief has no power.
Fear is a coward
of its own identity.
It can never win
without your permission.

*For the weapons of our warfare are not
carnal but mighty in God for pulling down
strongholds, casting down arguments and every
high thing that exalts itself against the
knowledge of God, bringing every thought
into captivity to the obedience of Christ and being
ready to punish all disobedience when your
obedience is fulfilled*

II Corinthians 10:4-6

Obvious

Standing in the middle
of an opened field.
He alone protects
and saves me.
My Defender,
my Shelter,
my Shield.
If the dew
or rain
shall happen to fall,
My rock of fortress
standing strong and tall.
As I look
upon the clear blue sky
a thought of heaven...
what will I see with the naked eye?
As I use my mind
to search behind
only to find
that our Prime Divine
sits on cloud nine,
drinking heavenly wine
heals the blind,

being kind
as He dines
and find time
to bind crime
as we wait in line
for our time.
Only to find
that the swine
cast a weapon to grind
our mind
to create a crime;
ignore the signs
that leaves you blind;
keeping in mind
that the High Divine
that you search to find
is right on
time.

God's love and protection
extends far beyond
life itself.
His beautiful blessings
are a blanket
of pleasure that covers pain,
despair, sickness, loneliness,
affliction, and sorrow.
He fulfills life with grace
and kindness
to provide the opportunity
to illustrate
His purpose.
Honor God's merits
by offering up
enthusiastic prayers of
thanksgiving and admiration.

And my God shall supply all your needs
according to His riches in glory by Christ
Jesus.
Philippians 4:13

Hello, God?

Talk to me
so that I can know
that you are there.
I know that you said
disobedience is so unfair,
I feel so bad
and I know within my heart
that I have done you wrong.
Knowing that this is the place
where you reside
and you alone,
but please come back home
where you belong.
Don't end our relationship
and consider it gone.
I need you now
more than ever before.
I count on you
when you take my hand
that leads to joy.
I will not give up
to sacrifice obedience.
You said to obey
is the main ingredient.

I admit
that I have sinned
and beg for your mercy,
so please don't turn your back
and be off in a hurry.
I have been punished
with guilt
and a great amount of shame.
There's only one thing left to do
as I stand in pain.
Confess my sins
unto your Holy and Righteous name.
Only you hold the key
of forgiveness
to unlock the door
to set me free.
As I turn the key to open the door,
you stand with opened arms
and me
with tears of joy.
Although it hurts,
confession works.
For I am not perfect,
nor am I worthy,
but I give you the victory and glory.

Conviction is the act of
confronting one in
their sins. During the time
you are wrapped in your
personal sin,
remember God can not
operate in it.
He is an active ingredient
of character that
directs or helps to reveal
your loss of innocence.
You must recognize your
violation and return
to your inevitable purpose.
Call upon the Lord and
He will grant repentance.

My Presence will go with you,
and I will give you rest.
Exodus 33:14

You are awakened
from a soft slumber that calmly
invades your soul.
This remarkable sensation yields
to the currents of radiance
that glides gracefully across
the threshold of your ripened nature.
It illuminates into perpetual bliss
that allows you to trust in God.
As you are being guided to seek
beyond the summit of your horizon,
even as God touches you within
the echoes of our mind;
He begins to murmur in the depths
of your conscience making perfection
on Earth a reality that is birth
from the canal of heaven.
A touch from God
sets you free to make you strong.

Chapter 6

Embraced By Love

Jeremy

The experiences of life
are so very natural.
Living the other side
is only spiritual.
Its like the passing
of a brand new day.
God will show up
and have His way.
You're come in our lives
for a moment or a season.
Don't know why
only God knows the real reason.
Your precious little beauty
would touch everyone you meet.
You had a special anointing
from your tender little head
to your precious, tiny feet.
Maybe that's why
you've come and gone so swift.
A touch of God's warm
kind heavenly bliss.
Can't avoid the feeling
that you will be missed.

Remembering your smiles
and laughter,
you were a great gift!
Perfect little angel
sent from above.
Born to all of us,
you were sent with love.
Challenges and trials
You never had to win.
Return to our Father God
above back in heaven.

Life and death is a part of God's plan of human requisite. We are all unique individuals created from God. Your life comprises of different avenues and adventures that are yet different from other human existences. Death marks an affirmation of value and a precious life on earth. Experience God's blessings of love, peace, and happiness. EXPERIENCE LIFE!

Whereas you do not know what will happen tomorrow.
For what is life? It is even a vapor that appears
for a little time and then vanishes away.
Instead you ought to say,
"If the Lord wills, we shall live and do this or that."
James 4:14-15

Pure Love

*Life
Is it a precious gift?
Don't reply to hasty,
fast or swift.
To respond to the question above.
Life.
Life is love.
Love is deep and centered within.
It's the opposite
of hatred, fear, and sin.
Love is more than just an emotion.
It's more than great affection, sex,
and devotion.
Love is something
that is preserved in you.
It's all righteous, pure, and true.
Can't be bought
nor found in another.
Love is in self.
Take your love
and love each other.
Awaken the beauty
that is hidden in you-
don't let anyone
define who you are
and what to do.*

Fill the void
of giving self-love.
Nurturing.
Love starts
by giving yourself
a hug.
Look in the mirror say
"I love myself".
Quiet your mind
and center yourself.
Love can be an addicting drug.
Other people can drain you
by feeding off your love.
Detoxify those
who are fending
with a repulsive urge.
Remove them from your life
and kick them to the curb.
Put God in your life
and develop a sense of self.
His constant love is there
and He'll love you,
all by Himself.

God designs life as a vehicle to
transport His spiritual
connection and applies
His everlasting love to embrace
His unique and creative
surroundings. Life exists
through the presence of
God's love.
God's genuine love is
a delightful gift granted for all.
It lies within the
innermost part of your soul...
YOUR HEART.

*For I am persuaded that neither death nor life, nor
angels, nor principalities, nor power, nor things present,
nor things to come, nor height, nor depth, nor any other
created thing, shall be able to separate us from the love
of God which is in Christ Jesus*
Romans 8:38-39

Lonely Heart

Having characteristics
of a widow.
I'm so tired of staying up at night
and crying on my pillow.
My heart feels the pain
of the emptiness.
Trying hard not to create
a moment of "self-pitiness."
Sad at the thought that I am alone.
Isolated,
dejected
this punishment feel so wrong!
Is there a drug that relieves
or lessen the pain?
Thinking in my mind
what would I obtain
or even gain
to keep from going insane.
Pray to the Master of Love.
As I lift my hands
waiting for falling blessings above.
Weeping endure for a night.
Stand on faith.
He'll make it all right.

Joy comes in the morning.
No more waking up in the mid-night
yawnin'.
As I stand
and wait on my Father
who never get tried.
Endure and steadfast
as I call myself
the "lone survivor".
I will stand apart and wait.
Longsuffering and faith
that's all it takes.
I will refuse to recognize
the heartahes
that keeps knocking at my mind.
I will trust
and believe God.
He will move that mountain.
It's a matter of time.
I will not give in
and I will keep pressing through.
For this pain
is only temporary
as I overcome this battle, too.

When you are withdrawn, recluse,
or secluded, you have made
the choice to be lonely.
Consolidate your time,
thoughts, and concerns along
with prayer to unite with God.
This connection will allow
you to become more secure
with yourself and strengthen
your self-reliance to become
companionable with God.
He detaches us from solitary
confinement, which eliminates
loneliness. You are never alone
with your associated
partner, God.

Yea, though I walk through the valley of the
shadow of death, I will fear no evil; For you are
with me; Your rod and your staff they comfort me.
Psalms 23:4

Weakness

Is it a sickness
or am I just plain weak to this.
When I declare to remain strong
I succumb to the ignorance
no matter how good it feels.
I know within my heart
I'm victim of wrong.
A given recognition
to the opposition
as I plead to the proposition
I'm required to make a decision
to this hypercritical vision.
Will I be forgiven
for what seems to be forbidden?
Call it all fiction
as I switch the position
using intuition.
God's given prescription
of forgiveness
take two dosage of submission
to release the tension
not to mention
my ammunition
that simulate my ambition
to carry out a discovered mission...

Weakness is the absence of
physical or moral strength.
Strength is coiled in the center
of your weakness.
It is firmly planted at the base
of your entire existence.
Strength begins to undergo
alterations through faith that God
supplies generously.
Having a personal relationship
with God extends your strength
from the core into outer limit
territory to produce an abundant
amount of power.   The entwined
power is a spiritual structure
for you to depend on.
God demonstrates His powers
through your weakness.
He uses His power to
protect, provide, and save.
Use your power as
a source of His strength.

Strengthen the weak hands, and make firm the feeble knees. Say to those who are fearful-hearted, "Be strong, do not fear!...He will come and save you."
Isaiah 35:3-4

The Best of the Best

You are the season of success,
a taste of self-determination
to start the process.
Never give up
as you continue to strive!
Do what it takes !
Put up a fight and
go that extra mile!
Always manage
to strive for the best,
with efforts of perseverance
that you must put behind a desk.
Don't surrender
and lose the battle
to fail the test.
Achieve from the depths
of your struggle
and don't settle for less.
You must know
that you are so very blessed.
I wish you much love,
peace, and happiness,
because you are the best of the best.

OH YES, THE BEST OF THE BEST!

You are a unique possession of
God's creation; a decorative
piece of jewel that is wonderfully
and fearfully designed through
the image of God.
It is through the self-sacrificed
act of His only begotten
son, Jesus, that compels
God to love us.
God provides the best for you,
because He loves you.
He loves you, because
He created you.
God's love is linked to
all facets of life that expands
to embrace all humanity.
You are the best,
because you come from
The Best!

Therefore I remind you to stir up the gift of God
which is in you...
2 Timothy 1:6

The heart and love is a parallel sytem
formatted to bring on
the existence of divine inspiration.
God lies at the axis of your heart.
He rotates His love in you
as it generates an endless flow of freedom.
As it travels along the shore
of your soul
it welcomes tears, happiness, fears,
frustration, determination, despondency,
hope, peace, enthusiasm, and joy.
Throughout this journey
you may encounter
different cycle of challenges,
but it never loses it path for adventure.
This intangible sense of power
is always brought back
to its original form
for you to freely embrace
as it captures the essence of your spirit.

Epilogue

I would weep, because my soul was crying
out for self-seeking love.
I would shed tears, because my spirit was suffering
from the lack of spiritual nourishment.
I would often grieve due to the fact
that my affirmations
were misguided, lost, and obscured
when confusion and hopelessness unexpectedly
presented itself.
Sinking in my mental miseries
and planning for a "Machiavellian" funeral
in hope to mourn over the burial of my struggles.
I found myself unrealistically pregnant.
There I was conceived by unpleasant thoughts
and low self-esteem that infringed on my true identity.
My labor pains were more intense,
because I carried fear and frustration
longer than a nine-month duration.
I began seeking God for guidance
and understanding in hopes to become liberated
from my oppressive attacks
that delighted in torture and destruction.
I became an acquaintance with my loneliness
and attempted to gain self-empowerment
through prayer.
Immediately I was isolated
from social cycles of friends, relatives, and family.
As I was placed in the middle of wilderness,
God helped me deliver my unwanted burdens.
Finally, I gave birth
to a new understanding of life,
releasing all fears and distress
that held me captive for so very long.

*I understood that healing was taking place
and freedom and faith were the advocators.
I am now renewed into the
image of divine purity as
I accept and release love that
is generating in my soul, my mind, and my spirit.
In the midst of my obstacles and shortcomings,
I knew that I will never be alone,
because God is my source of strength.
God is positioned above, to watch over me.
God is beneath, sustaining me.
God is near, to protect me.
God is in front, behind, and inside of me.
He is in total control
as He directs and secures my path.
Let there be any form of adversities
and I know that I am covered,
because the presence of God is my shield.
I am embraced by the love of God
and so are you!
Stay strong and prayerful.*

Humbly yours,

So'Nia

Embracing Your Thoughts

The Lord knows the thoughts of man
Psalm 94:11